ARNOSKY'S ARK

JIM ARNOSKY

NATIONAL GEOGRAPHIC SOCIETY
Washington, D.C.

To create his paintings Jim Arnosky
used acrylics in an opaque oil technique
on bristol board.

Published by the
National Geographic Society
1145 17th Street N.W.
Washington, D.C. 20036

Library of Congress Cataloging-in-Publication Data
Arnosky, Jim
          Arnosky's ark / by Jim Arnosky.
                    p.   cm.
          Summary: In paintings and text the author
describes his feelings about a variety of animals and
explains the threats each species has faced and what can
be done to protect them.
          ISBN 0-7922-7112-2
          1. Animals—Miscellanea—Juvenile
literature. 2. Animals—Pictorial works—
Juvenile literature.
[1. Animals—Miscellanea. 2. Wildlife conservation.]
I. Title.
QL49.A766   1999
590—dc21   98-54601

Printed in U.S.A.

For Olivia

Introduction

Hi. I'm Jim Arnosky, and this book is my ark. In it I've included many of my favorite animals. Some are old friends — animals I see often, write about, and paint pictures of nearly every day. There are also new friends I've met and enjoyed on my travels to wild places.

We live in a wondrous time. Attitudes and ideas about the Earth and its creatures are shifting, changing for the better. Our understanding of the natural world is broadening. We are slowly learning to share space and live with other species. More and more, we care whether the wildlife we have come to know throughout this century will be with us in the next.

People have come a long way in their relationships with wild animals. We still have a way to go. Many species totter on the edge of a terrible chasm, their very existence endangered. Is there hope for them? I think so.

A number of the animals considered quite common today were threatened or endangered species a hundred years ago. Some of these I have chosen to put in my ark. They are animals whose survival stories I think you should know, along with the stories of a few other animals that are endangered now and whose numbers are dwindling.

With a new century close ahead, I wondered what I could do to celebrate the occasion. I decided I would offer some perspective by looking back over the past one hundred years, at least half of which I have seen for myself. The conservation movement, which began in the 19th century and which has resulted in the creation of our national parks and wildlife refuges, has blossomed into the current environmental awareness. Today, it is abundantly clear that each small act of kindness toward the natural world helps better the environment in which we all live. This ark is my small act of kindness for the animals I love most.

Jim Arnosky
Ark 2000

The beaver is the first animal I put in my ark because I spend more time watching beavers than I do watching any other wild animal. Where I live, beavers are abundant. We have beavers in our tiny brook. We can watch them from our kitchen window. Each year I see a few new beaver dams and ponds established. I have no doubt our beavers will be with us in the 21st century. But a hundred years ago the beavers' future was insecure. They had been nearly wiped out by the relentless trapping fueled by the demand for their luxurious fur, which was used primarily in making men's hats.

People concerned about beavers' dwindling numbers took up the animals' cause and worked to pass laws protecting them. The beavers were protected and slowly increased their numbers. It took three decades for them to reestablish themselves throughout their range.

Government protection helped save beavers from possible extinction, but credit must also go to the beavers themselves. Anyone who has watched a beaver beginning a new dam, arranging small sticks across a fast-flowing stream, can easily imagine the animal refusing to go away, stubbornly persisting against any and all odds.

ison deserve a place in my ark because they stand as an example of our most shameful behavior toward wildlife. In the 19th century bison were mercilessly slaughtered for their meat, hides, and bones, which were crushed into fertilizer. They were also killed for sport by marksmen shooting from windows of moving trains.

By 1880 the bison, which had for centuries provided food and clothing to Native Americans, had been reduced from close to 60 million animals to less than a thousand. Today, after twelve decades of protection, there are fewer than 250,000 bison in the United States. All of them live on carefully managed preserves or in private herds. We can never witness the spectacle of the original herd. We will never know what it was like to hear the thunder of millions of bison hooves pounding the earth.

In the 1950s, when I was a young boy, every adventure I imagined had a great big dangerous alligator. I had never seen a real live alligator. I saw them in movies and on TV. In magazines there were pictures of baby alligators being sold as mail-order pets. I don't know what people did with them. Most likely the alligators died in captivity. Around the same time, ladies carried handbags made from the skins of young alligators, with alligator heads, legs, and feet sewn into the design. It was also fashionable to have shoes, belts, and wallets made of alligator skin, and whole alligators were stuffed for display on mantelpieces. It wasn't long before the alligator products outnumbered the alligators.

In 1973 Congress passed the Endangered Species Act, and alligators became a protected species. Poaching and illegal trade in alligator hides continued. But under protection, alligators were able to increase their numbers. I have seen for myself how well a protected species can do. In 1970, while bicycling many miles on the back roads of southern Florida, I saw only one large alligator. In 1993, on an auto trip across south Florida, my wife, Deanna, and I were able to see a large alligator in nearly every highway culvert pool. Alligator products, from meat to leather goods, are still being sold. But these days they come from special alligator farms and from controlled hunting of any excess in the wild population. In my work I have been able to visit the wonderfully wild places where alligators live. And every trip into alligator country has been a real-life adventure.

Never as numerous as alligators, American crocodiles have not been able to adapt to the changes brought about by human encroachment. When the crocodiles suffered threats to their existence, they did not rebound well. Today, American crocodiles are found mostly in the southernmost part of Florida on the edges of Florida Bay. The large crocodile pictured here is an exception. It left Florida Bay and swam many miles up the Gulf of Mexico to Sanibel, Florida, where it took up residence in the Ding Darling National Wildlife Refuge. The crocodile was captured and returned to Florida Bay, only to swim all the way back up the Gulf to Sanibel again. There it has stayed, the only crocodile in the refuge.

Cougar, panther, puma, catamount, and mountain lion are all names for the same animal. When Europeans first set foot on this continent, cougars were plentiful. They were in the woods, swamps, and mountains. Early settlers were fearful of cougars and shot them on sight. There was little use for the meat or the hide. The cougars were killed simply to get rid of them. When a species is targeted for annihilation and its population is destroyed, it is said to be extirpated.

By 1900, after centuries of persecution, the cougar had been extirpated from much of its eastern range. Since then, the last stronghold of North America's largest wild cat has been the rugged mountains of the West. But now, at the close of the 20th century, the western cougars are being threatened. They are losing habitat and having their hunting grounds encroached upon by human populations.

Cougars need a lot of room to roam and hunt. They can travel a great distance in a day's time. There is some indication that they migrate from one part of the country to another. Every year sightings of cougars are reported in places where they had not been seen for many, many years.

I put the cougar in my ark because I am convinced that cougars have recently been in and have taken up residence in my home state of Vermont. I've found and followed their tracks on not one but two occasions.

I like big animals because they need lots of space. I know that in order to have a bear population, for example, there have to be vast wooded areas for the bears to roam. I put the black bear in my ark because it is a favorite of mine and because it represents our wildest, most rugged, and remote places.

Black bears are woodland animals. Large numbers of black bears roamed through the woods that covered much of the continent before the arrival of Europeans. Settlers found the bears in abundance. Black bears were killed for food, fur, and for their grease, which was used in cooking and to burn in lamps. As the trees were cleared for homes and farms, the bears retreated deeper into the forest.

As people moved West, more and more woodland was cleared, further shrinking bear habitat. Black bears still lived throughout most of their original range but in far fewer numbers. They might have been pressed close to extinction had it not been for the preservation of the wilderness areas into which a good many bears had retreated. The first of these was Yellowstone National Park. Throughout the 20th century other national parks have been established, setting aside more and more land that provides ideal habitat for bears. If bears have enough woodland to roam in, they will thrive.

My home is surrounded by wooded hills, and we have a healthy population of black bears. To paint this picture, I went into those hills to a high ridge where many beech trees grow. Almost every tree there is scarred by the claws of bears climbing to eat the beechnuts.

The black bear survived the onslaught of civilization by avoiding human beings. White-tailed deer, on the other hand, have thrived in our midst. There are more deer now than there were a hundred years ago. At the turn of the last century deer populations were very low. It wasn't the deforestation of the 1800s that hurt deer — the best thing you can do for deer is clear away some trees so underbrush, the deer's food, can grow. It was hunters who, after the Civil War, began shooting the then abundant deer and selling the meat in markets. Venison, as deer meat is called, was and still is a good food. But the market hunting of any wild animal can lead to wholesale slaughter. This is what happened to deer and is what caused their numbers to drop drastically.

A ban on market hunting and controls on the number of deer killed by individual hunters reconstituted the herd. Then, as the 20th century landscape slowly developed into a patchwork of woods, fields, stonewalls, hedgerows, roads, and highways, the transformation favored deer. Deer love edgelands where they can graze in the open sunlight and dash for safety into nearby brush and woods. This is why deer are even found living around housing developments. The edges created by residential lawns, woodlots, and undeveloped fields give deer all they need, and they move in. The white-tailed deer in my painting is one I saw within the city limits of Philadelphia. It lives in the woods and fields surrounding a factory.

The deer is the most important animal in my ark because it presents us with a challenge. In the 21st century we will have to not only protect wild animals, but also learn to live with them. We'll have to be willing to give them their share of land and tolerate their trespassing onto ours.

All my life I have sung the praises of trout — rainbow, brown, and brook trout. But the truth is, I love the brook trout most. In the hemlock-covered mountains of Pennsylvania, I caught my first brook trout. It was fat and heavy. Its back was forest green, and its fins were a brilliant red. It was a wild fish in a wild stream. The water was ice cold. Brook trout need cold water to survive.

Throughout the 19th century, as trees were cut down to make farmland, more and more sections of the native eastern brook trout's streams were opened to sunlight. Naturally, the water warmed, forcing the trout to crowd into the colder pockets and pools. But soon even those retreats were too warm, and the brook trout suffered and died.

Rather than restore the brook trout's habitat, steps were taken by some pioneer fish biologists to supplant the fading native brook trout with trout

more tolerant to warmer water.
In 1882 the first shipment of brown
trout eggs arrived from Europe. After a brief period of
failure, the transplanted brown trout began to take hold. Soon, many cold,
ancestral brook trout waters became warmer brown trout streams.

We still have wild, native brook trout, but they can only be found in our
coldest, clearest mountain streams. I like brown trout. They are undeniably
beautiful creatures. But in the future when we're faced with a choice between
restoring a wild animal's habitat or simply replacing the animal with one
more tolerant to change, I hope we will choose restoration.

f all the birds of prey, ospreys are my favorite. I love the way they fly high over the water and suddenly dive, plunging to catch a fish. For my ark I chose a family of ospreys that had built their great nest high atop a platform specially provided for them in a wildlife sanctuary.

People have not always been so kind to ospreys. Well into the 20th century ospreys, hawks, and other birds of prey were considered vermin. The birds were shot out of the sky for fun. Finally, in the 1930s, this kind of slaughter drew the attention of conservationists, and the first bird of prey sanctuary was established in Pennsylvania at a place called Hawk Mountain.

By the mid-20th century a different kind of threat emerged. A widely used chemical pesticide known as DDT was discovered to be contaminating water and fish. Ospreys and many other fish-eating birds suffered from DDT poisoning, ingesting small doses with every fish eaten.

Once enough of the chemical had accumulated in a bird's system, it caused the bird's eggshells to be so thin that the eggs broke before any baby birds could hatch! Eventually the use of DDT was banned. Dedicated people incubated eggs, raised and released birds, and provided suitable sites for the released birds to nest to help these endangered species make a comeback.

For some species of wildlife even the slightest change in their environment can have immediate, shocking results. For the temperature-sensitive Florida manatee, a temporary chilling of their warm-water habitat can kill. Manatees are extremely vulnerable to pneumonia. Manatees also have been known to die suddenly from mysterious causes.

One not so mysterious cause of manatee deaths is the injuries they receive from boat propellers. I have watched manatees swimming slowly in their shallow rivers. It is easy to see how a passing motorboat can accidentally strike these creatures. To help reduce the numbers of accidental injuries to manatees, boaters must reduce their speed and move carefully through manatee areas. The number of Florida manatees is estimated to be 1,850. I put this gentle giant in my ark because if we lose the manatee — because of disease, injury, or loss of habitat — the world in the 21st century will be less one wonder.

At the beginning of this century we knew little about whales beyond how to hunt and kill them efficiently. For 19th-century whalers, subduing an animal many times their size out in the open ocean took bravery and great skill. But just as remarkable an achievement, and one which also takes bravery and skill, is going out to sea to learn how whales live. Today, people are doing this, and the knowledge they have gained has been instrumental in protecting many whales from overhunting and in saving whole species of whales from extinction.

The more we learn about whales, the more apparent it becomes that they possess an intelligence that equals or may, in fact, exceed our own.

Like the great whales in their darkest times, sharks are being slaughtered wantonly and wastefully. Our knowledge of sharks and their importance to ocean life is severely limited by our fear of them. The shark is in my ark because I am convinced that the next century will illuminate the shark just as this passing century has shed light on the whale.

ife on Earth is endlessly evolving. Every species soon will have another century of development enfolded into its genetic bank. How many species are yet to be discovered? How many have we lost? Glance backward with me once more over the past one hundred years to the horizon that was the year 1900. In the span of time between that distant, faded line and the present moment, the mountain gorilla was discovered then feared, vilified, killed, persecuted, threatened by extinction, observed, studied, protected, and today appreciated and even loved. It shouldn't take a century for us to learn the truth about an animal and care about its welfare. We can do better. We need to do much better.

Like Noah, who built the biblical ark, I too was constrained by size. I could not squeeze all my concerns, hopes and respect for wild animals into one small book. Fortunately, my heart has love enough for all the Earth's wildlife, and my mind can hold every creature I see.

I invite you to make your own ark — a book like mine, or perhaps a model or cutout of an ark like Noah's. Then fill it with your own favorite animals. They may be animals from any place in the world — tigers, snakes, parrots, butterflies — whatever animals you wish. Draw them and paint them. Write something you have learned about each one. Then make it your business to care about what happens to them.

If enough of you make arks filled with animals, the whole world of wildlife may get safely aboard with lots of caring people watching over them.

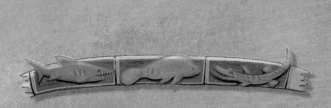